Two Stars

Reflections of a
Military Wife and Mother

By

Victoria Ventura

ISBN-10 0-9988249-3-3
ISBN 13 978-0-9988249-3-2

Copyrights © 2016, © revised 2017 by Victoria Ventura

All rights reserved. No part of this publication may be reproduced, distributed, or transmitted in any form or by any means, including photocopying, recording, or other electronic or mechanical methods, without the prior written permission of the publisher, except in the case of brief quotations embodied in critical reviews and certain other noncommercial uses permitted by copyright law.

Printed in the United States of America.

Dedication

I would like to dedicate this book to my husband, son and daughter and all the other pilots and soldiers and families who have dedicated their lives to our country in one way or another. These stories are based on true events of pilots and soldiers in different war zones from Vietnam, Afghanistan, and Iraq.

I would also like to thank all my friends and teachers who were instrumental in helping me get published. And lastly to all my dear friends Bill and the late Ray, who were so supportive of me and my family during stressful war times with prayers and support. It made these times more bearable and positive. I love you all.

I am writing about the military because words can paint pictures that come alive of past experiences. They are like movies of the mind, the scenes that portray soldiers and their families in real life experiences whether at home, protecting foreign countries to establish a democracy, flying combat missions and being in com-bat on the ground. The idea of the cute Vietnam young lady twirling a flag that covers her from all the elements of war, to a Firefight pinning down Army Rangers on a hill by the Taliban and then being protected by "Big Bird'(an AC-130 Specter Gunship), gives us visions of being safe while being pinned down in a dangerous crossfire. You can feel the sadness and hear the tears and the tension in Arlington's slow and methodical parade to the last resting sight of a soldier's graveside. This is followed by the bursting of explosive laughter at the simplicity of the horses' antics at such a serious event. I hope that these experiences will give a deeper understanding to the military life of soldiers and their families as they live day to day at home, overseas deployed in foreign countries or in dangerous war zone.

Acknowledgements

My thanks to the following individuals who helped with the content or the language of this chap-book: Vivian Shipley, a great poet and empowering, inspirational teacher, Jeff Mock, a great poet and teacher who helped me with the nuts and bolts and Christine Beck, a great poet who first saw my work and encouraged me.

I also want to recognize my deceased husband who flew the tiniest single engine reconnaissance air-craft Cessna (O2), in the most dangerous places during the Vietnam War, my daughter who was an accomplished P-3 pilot for the US Navy flying covert missions throughout the world and my son who received the Distinguished Flying Cross for repeatedly flying his lumbering AC-130 gunship into a firefight against the Taliban and Al-Qaeda. One incident was the saving Marines in a firefight during a sandstorm with one engine down. Another was protecting ground troops pinned down on a mountain for several days. This resulted in saving all 84 wounded US military personnel. He and his crew were awarded a place on the Mackay Trophy at the Smithsonian for the "most meritorious flight of the year". Previous recipients include Eddie Rickenbacker, Jimmy Doolittle and Chuck Yeager.

I would like to remember my good friend Ray D'Alessio, who first read my book with love and encouraged me to keep going. And finally to my best friend and critic, Bill who inspires me every day to see life with love, wisdom and faith in all my writing.

TWO STARS

I love poetry – reading, writing, hearing, and speaking. My final thought in offering my poetic reflections on a mother's experience in and with our military is to take a small step to bring two elements together – everyday civilian life and my other parallel universe. Since the all-volunteer service these elements have drifted apart. I worry that it is unhealthy for our society. An overwhelming number of families now have no direct participation in an experience that has been commonplace and essential throughout our history. Lack of awareness increases uninformed decisions. Perhaps artistic expression can affect the drift.

TESTIMONIALS

"Victoria Ventura is a poet at heart trying to join the two major threads of her life, her everyday civilian life and that as the wife and mother of three members of the professional military. While she is the widow of a now deceased Vietnam veteran, both her daughter and her son also served as professional military aviators. She worries that the all-volunteer military service has driven traditional family elements apart and both civilian and military families suffer accordingly.

One is reminded of Sybil Stockdale, recently deceased widow of Admiral James B Stockdale, who became a model for military spouses across the armed services, demonstrating that military families often bear as much of a burden as our professional warriors. Read Victoria's poetry, it will take you back to Vietnam and introduce Iraq, Afghanistan and other conflicts from the Middle East."

Jon A. Reynolds
Brig Gen, US Air Force (Ret)
Vietnam POW

"I originally read your poems when you sent them last month and took some time to reflect on them. I can't imagine how it made you feel and after reading it, it makes me realize a bit of what my own mother was feeling and I feel bad for putting her though that. I'm not the type to dwell on my military experience and I kind of keep in as much of my past as I can. Reflecting on Victoria's poetry of a mother's experience with children in the military, I have a deeper awareness of my own mother's feelings."

U.S. Army Sgt. Daniel Laffin
Afghanistan 2006 - 2008

"*Reflections of a Military Wife and Mother* is a wonderful group of short poems that spans the gaps of branch and periods served. It encompasses feelings soldiers, sailors, airmen and marines have post deployments in any area, and how their time served affects their loved ones. *Dark Life* hits home the feelings of lost battles to PTSD and to friends who mentally never came home and their struggles to be normal again."

SSG Robert Laffin
U.S. Army 2001 – 2012

Contents

DEDICATION	III
ACKNOWLEDGEMENTS	V
TESTIMONIALS	7
911	12
COMBAT ZONES	14
MILITARY MEN EVERYWHERE	17
FIRESTORM	20
WARTIME MEMORIES OF A WIFE, MOTHER	24
IN COUNTRY	27
TET	29
CHINOOK	31
MUSIC MAN	33
THE WALL	34
THE AMERICANIZATION OF PEACE	38
THE DEACON	40
MISSING	41
ARMY MOTHER'S PRAYER	42
FLYING OVER HOME	45
FIREFIGHT	46
WINGS, WINGS, WINGS	49
DAVID AND GOLIATH	51

A SNIPER'S FAVORITE MOTHER'S SHOT	53
PRECIOUS DAUGHTER IN FLIGHT	55
JIHAD JOHN	56
THE STONING	59
BELOVED CHILD	60
OVERSEAS AGAIN?	62
ACTIVE DUTY	63
GROUNDHOG DAY	65
IDF (ISRAELI DEFENSE FORCE)	66
THE GIRLS	67
THE CATS	69
MIXED TEA BAGS	70
PICTURE PERFECT	72
THREE MEN	73
A LITTLE TWINKLE	74
GRANDMA, I AM HOME	76
MAMMA, MAY I?	79
WAR EAGLES	81
BLUE ANGELS	83
SPIRIT UPRISING	86
THE DARK LIFE	87
THE CEMETERY	88
TAPS	89
TRANSCENDENCE	91
ROCK	93
WALKING ON SCRUFFY TURF	94

ARLINGTON	96
POPPIES	99
ORDER FORM	101

911

On stage, talking to students
about future military careers.
Showering words of wisdom,
when I was escorted
out of the auditorium.

Watching TV
seeing planes
crashing, metal splintering
as showering toothpicks
falling thousands of feet.

King Kong?
Gone wrong?

Smoke, fire
pouring, while
miniature
spider people flying,
to nowhere.

Dust clouds
descending into
tunneled streets,
New York City, underground.

Dust settles,
buildings gone,
people ashed,
voices daunting
saying goodbye, so long.

Then silence,
hear the silence?
Listen to the silence.
Hear the phones ringing?

9/11/01

Combat Zones

Alert! Alert! Alert!
The text message sings its song,
bell ringing on the phone
Get out! Get out! Get out!

What a terrible thing to live in fear,
but so many of our worries are trivial
compared to some.
A very selective few people know true terror,
death stalks my son!

Threat! Threat! Threat!
Hide, Hide, Hide,
No safety anywhere,
another school closed,
bomb scare or fire drill.
Who knows what evil lies there?

He knows not how the Grim Reapers eye,
came to rest on him as he flies,
though he can feel
its unblinking stare.
Ever pressing on his soul,
trying to bring him down from the sky!

Every day another scare,
children calling in threats.
To avoid the inevitable action
knives slashing,
guns smoking, machine
gun ripping bursts, we know not where?

Its dark presence continuously
haunts his life,
he knows not where it will strike,
on the ground or in the air?
Forced to live in constant vigilance of all,
his only protection, prayers to an uncaring God.

Carnage falling
like dead soldiers,
body parts flying,
a finger here,
a toe there,
blood squirting in the air
innocents dead?

You say you know fear and woe,
but I say to you
that you can't have
even the slightest clue,

TWO STARS

of what true terror is,
flying low in a war zone.
Death stalks my son.

What sense does this make?
Gentle Souls flying
to their sacred place!
A world awake

Too,

Too,

Late!

Military Men Everywhere

Old solders never die,
they don't even fade away?
They just stay and say;

"Been there, Done that,"
World War Two, Vietnam,
Desert Storm.

Other places, I cannot mention,
all ages everywhere, but not here,
coming together to hear old stories.

Posturing their tales of long ago,
who's alive, who's dead?
Life goes on to march ahead.

Military men all ages everywhere,
all times, centuries, wars past
coming together to hear the old stories
each other posturing their tales of long
ago.

Marching to Nowhere

I see them all in a row,
yelling their drill songs,Parris Island,
you know,
marching for twenty miles
or more,
as the blistering hot sun comes
sweltering, beating them down,
putting each soldier
in dismay.

I see them holding their own,
walking with blistery,
squishy feet,
feeling that 103 degree heat!

No talking, I hear only
the crunching sound of bones,
as they march in cadence,
each one alone.

Unbeknownst to you or me,
I think, where are you going
my soldier, my son?
Why are you marching in the hot, hot
sun?

God protect you every day,
as you're gone
until you come home.
Once more in my arms.

Firestorm

She listens to the thunder
of rockets shooting off,
to hear the conversation of others saying,
"It takes twenty minutes for
new lieutenants to die In Country," Vietnam.

She thinks of him
waiting for those cookies
that come only in crumbs
in a shoebox packed with aluminum
layered ever so delicately,
with wax paper, only
to come as crumbs with melted chocolate chips.

She sends a tape. With songs
telling of events, news of home in
the states.
A sense of normality
while the Mamasans steal his Gruen watch.

As inbound comes from Marble
Mountain, he hits the floor
with the mattress over his
head to be comforted by

the dog he feeds with his rations.
Next day he takes the general flying
for the ride of his life.

As the general commands
him to do the regular flight pattern,
while flying the sortie, the enemy ground fire
nearly hits his plane.

The general decides
the experienced
pilot, who has no casualties as yet,
may be correct in
the new flight path
that gets the job done.

Life is quiet at home
with no fear of death,
as the men in Nam who come home
shaking with Agent Orange
or wearing the clothes of
dead comrades?

TWO STARS

They are the survivors for
death changes their
lives forever.
Nothing has changed.
Men come home,
not quite right.

But always ready

To fight for:

Freedom,

God,

Country,

Family.

O-2 Skymaster reconnaissance plane DaNang, Vietnam (My husband's plane.)

Wartime Memories of a Wife, Mother

He comes back from Vietnam,
a different man
with self-hatred and disgust
to the napalm war of burnt bodies
in villages and rice paddies.

No PTSD here!
No one knew
that erratic behaviors
were never you.
Children stealing watches,
Mamasans leaving bombs,
in hooch's of men friends
No more.

Stories of inbound all around,
crawling on the ground,
while you dive under your bed,
with mattresses over your head.

Your new friend,
a scraggly mutt by your side,
huddling and shaking,
protecting your head.

No talking about his stay, only wants to get away.
Getting married and never see those paper plates again.
Until the honeymoon and the side trip to an island,
where a beach picnic turns into a tailspin of anger
and hands in air shouting,
no more paper plates again!

All go flying like saucers into the air!
look and stare, very aware.
She goes to hug him and wraps her arms around
sinewy shoulders,
only to be put in a head lock of death,
as she yells, "Honey it's me!"

Years later and another war,
joking at dinner one starry, starry Christmas night,
a daughter announces that flying over her brother,
"I could have bombed you as you fly at night!"
Choking back my horror as I eat a bite.

Now, her father Arlington buried,
not too far from her pilot friends.
Blown up, or shot down
a few feet away so she cannot
visit her father's grave.

TWO STARS

Sitting with her friend,
slashed from ear to ear,
I stare as we eat Mexican,
wondering twelve or fourteen inches.
Oh dear! Scars that can't be hidden
on a Mr. Clean shaven head.

A mother sits and waits to see,
are they coming home in one piece
or fractured into many of the unseen?
PTSD is the "Wounded Warrior" scene.

In Country

I am the man
walking forty
years hence from
Hanoi Hilton
to a lovely rolling hill.
Visiting old friends
paying respects
to those who never made it home.
Smelling that earthy,
green, brown ground,
new soil just opened.
Remembering the leeches
in my shoes,
sucking my life blood out.
Vermin everywhere in the
wet tall grass.
Now seeing and enjoying the view
from the hillcrest that
lead to a beautiful view of cherry blossom trees,
and a gold dome amongst
thatched brown huts,
spreading into terraced, rice fields.
I feel the blustering
wind blowing like

old time Cong banshees
on the hill.
Gusting and hiding through the
branches saying,

"Lay at rest, rest
the final rest."

TET

Horrible sights for all to see.
No one should be
exposed to these. He sees
it all and tells for years about
experiences

No one should bear.
Tet offensive fighting on a hill.
Man falling over, his dog is killed.
He tells of stealing pants, combat boots
too,

that won't be used by dead corpses
along the routes. Getting the stench off.
No baths for days, skin is black.
Will it ever be the same?

He thinks going home, can't wait to be
normal again and be with thee.
He tells his story for years to come.
No student should ever be on the run.

TWO STARS

He teaches about a time so true
that men were not men but trying to be
true blue.

Country he served and proud of
his honor. He shares with students
what it means to be a soldier.

Combat is real and killing is true.
No one should have to give his due.

Chinook

Seated perched, high
in the air, dangling over the side,
looking down at the towns,
with rice paddies and the
one road that I fly over,
covered with
Snakes.

Snakes could be the enemy.
I swoop and don't know what
I am aiming at. Hidden in the
water ready to attack, I
pull back and wait.

The enemy waits, too.
I am the invader.
This is his land and town
so we wait until we can
attack, not ever sure if we
can win the war.

TWO STARS

Chinook helicopter with machine gunners

Music Man

I worked with him for
years, never knowing who
or what he really was until tonight.

A music teacher in middle school
with a two hundred piece band!
Turned counselor, later on.

He always said, "You can't put ten pounds of potatoes
in a five pound sack."

Where did he get this from?
A man who helped others
willingly in the Christian way,
who went to Nam as a gunner?
On a Chinook?

Who plays on his keyboard
at nursing homes?
Who shoots baskets?
Who talks of war as a year of his life?
And learned, look busy and keep your
mouth shut and don't volunteer.

TWO STARS

Vietnam Memorial Wall, Washington, DC

The Wall

(thoughts on a dear friend)

The Wall speaks for itself of
valor and acts beyond the Greek gods
of old. Many speak their names,
Ray, William, John, Butch, Dennis,
not remembering,
how they became part
of this Black Monument.

Each telling his story
of "In Country" heroics or
just trying to stay alive, jumping out
of hellos or fighting on
the ground dug in tunnels.
Praying and holding on to their helmets
while clutching their armor
around their mud drenched jungle bodies.

The beginnings of Saint Michael
against Lucifer, cutting
down the warriors against mankind.
Wielding his sword, swashing the wrongs
of all the evil beings' actions.

TWO STARS

In the blackness of night,
with only the moon lighting The Wall,
whispers can be heard like the
water in the gardens of nearby fountains,
bubbling with excitement, discussing what
they saw that day, who came to visit and
what did they have to say. Flowers, stuffed animals
and pins left with the tears of family and friends.

Mumbling tearful prayers as they dab away
the mascara from their eyes.
And the Names ask, "When is it my turn to visit?"

Names of Vietnam Veterans on Memorial Wall

The Americanization of Peace
(Coming of Age)

Four foot five flag girl
Vietnamese child,
waving her six foot red, white and blue
flag over her head.

The "Colors" flying
twirling the "Stars and Stripes."
Perfection her goal in life.
Around her head as the stars are to
Polaris,
circling in perfect synchronization.

I watched her grow embracing
the American way, with all ninety-five
pounds of inspiration to all she touches.
With her ever giving energy, faith
and beliefs of unselfish love.

A flickering candle giving constant life
in a storm, ever inspiring others,
shining in her celestial glow.

Putting to rest any war
that is never quite right.

Sending the beacon of hope and
belief that we are all at peace.
Love for our countries in all
their beauty as she becomes
an American by speech.

The Deacon

The Deacon was a large man,
six feet four, a humble presider at my son's
Military Wedding. So large was he in character,
full of laughter and life and that at the close of the service
he belted out unexpectedly the song, "I believe",
dear to my heartstrings as memories came flooding back
of my father singing this song of boundless love,
blessing my son's marriage from up above.
Deacon was a retired Air Force man of World War II,
special in his own right as a Tuskegee Airman blessing another
pilot on this day to celebrate life.
Always smiling and positive praying
Mary's prayers to shower upon us graces for our children.

(He now sings in the heavenly Chorus of Choruses.)

Missing

I watched my son leave
on a plane to Afghanistan
war has just begun, again
his squadron is being deployed.

On a plane to Afghanistan
eyes down, my heart bleeding,
war has just begun, again.
Who will return home?

Eyes down, my heart bleeding,
many go into the zone.
Who will return home?
Wounded warriors, all alone?

Many go into the zone coming back home
wounded warriors, all alone?
Cracked heads or PTSD instead?

Coming back home
I wait by the phone
Cracked heads or PTSD instead?
Prayers answered, he is back home!

Army Mother's Prayer

(Pantoum on War)

Who are we? Sitting, waiting,
Praying, rocking
Women of all sects, religions and sizes.
Moslem, Jewish, Catholic, Protestant.
No differences here.

We see time standing still
We assemble, rocking as
I think and meditate.
We fear that I may see her or him
beheading in God's Holy Name?
We imagine what will his fate deliver?
What will become of my child?

Time has a way of passing slowly.
We sit as eyes glisten
In dead calm dismay,
The days depressed,
menacing clouds
falling rain
cannot cleanse the doom.

What will happen?
We sit,
pray,
wait,
For our children
who may come home
from his or hers hellish state.

TWO STARS

AC- 130 Gunships (my son's plane)

Flying Over Home

(AC-130 Gunships)

Out of nowhere
I hear
the sound of that
unforgettable hum, drum
drum, groan,
of four engines.

Flying, flying so low
droning that
tune, tuning,
drumming that Song
from years gone by.

Bellying home
on those wings
of love to keep
us safe
from all the unknown.

Firefight

I saw a flag
unfurling in the breeze,
ruffling sounds, chanting.
Freedom is not Free!

Encased on a mantle
another flag, unfolding its story,
quietly sings
of 84 saved, ambushed, living soldiers.

They huddled in trenches
on a mountaintop,
for three days
lightning gun fires, brightening tracers,
between God and evil.

A large night bird flies,
protecting with gunship power.
Specter's its name.
Sending hope
for tomorrow.

Men standing,
chanting in
nighttime blackness.

Waving arms at
the big bird's body,
sweeping, swooping
down dragon fire that stops the enemy.

All 84
wounded rangers.
Stars and Stripes
on arms, from
a raging firefight.

While a dying father,
hears courageous deeds by
his returned son, whispering
to his wife,
"Your son is a damn hero."

TWO STARS

AC 130H- Gunship fires flares

Wings, Wings, Wings
(And not chicken Wings either?!)

Wings in Nam,
aviators flying fifty years of fun,
one will be a Top Gun.

Khe Sanh Valley on the run
"Covey Fac" sign, sung by one.
Call sign "Snoopy,"
a man who will be the father of two
heroic pilots, who knew?

Sleeps in Arlington
under a bed of grass,
with a stone pillow
for his head.

A son flying over
war zone again.
This time Afghanistan
To save those troops
from definite doom.

Droning sounds of gunship at night,
his old name, "Puff the Magic Dragon" on sight.

TWO STARS

"Grim Reaper," new name now, brings safety to all
for troops getting inbound in dangerous Firefight.

A daughter flying
quietly low, bringing
safety to all scouring lands to protect
all below.
And trophies too,
shared in Smithsonian
with Rickenbacker too!

Proud Dad watching
from above, letting
his light keep them safe in love.
Always last words,

"FLY SAFE

"BE SAFE"

(Love Mom and Dad)

David and Goliath

Based in Afghanistan,
running alone inside
the outermost fence,
where I didn't belong
peaceful, free, safe
serotonin flowing.

Doing my five-mile stretch
around the perimeter of
Baghdad Air Base,
trying to stay in
shape. With cricks,
flying takes its toll
on my body and soul.
Sitting thirteen hours
flying in circles every night
makes the butt,
sore and stiff, feeling the breezes
and not seeing, squinting
as the sand blows in my face and eyes.

It happened, a hit
then another, temple shots!

TWO STARS

A rock by what? A ten your old boy? Slingshots rocks,
his ammo, stinging my head. Saying,
"Allah Akbar" as a group
of older men encouraging, watching,
smiling, rocking, nodding saying "Mohammed be praised!"
I say "Jesus Christ,"
let me be safe!

Seeing the lookout tower
with the gunnies
on high, watching,
I fly, feet double, quadrupled
timed.

Praying safety on my side,
I climb up
the 200-foot tower
the roar of smoke bombs
to dispel the newly gathered crowd.

Hearing comrades
telling me
don't worry,
"Happens all the time.
Hole in fence you know."

A Sniper's Favorite Mother's Shot

A mother sits
sees,
a shooting star,
shooters at the bar.

How many drinks
do I shoot to?
See the outcome
of her man-boy.

On a roof
deciding,
who should live?
Who should die?

Locked into a shot,
stopper of tequila
and beer,
seeing the scene
of her son,
waiting, watching, frying,
in Mosul disguise,
pulling a trigger.

TWO STARS

Who will live?
Who will die?

A legend in
his own right,
not knowing the
bounty on his head!

Precious Daughter in Flight

Another child
daughter,
Beauty Queen,
Runway Model!

Navy pilot,
flying over brother
by God,
knows whose design?

War zone strategy
protecting country,
if daughter captured,
tortured and
will beheaded mine?

Orion P3 (My daughter's plane)

Jihad John
(Militant)

Regular name,
Regular life,
coming of age
Sad sinister.

Westminster,
London,
brought up
with three others.

Taxicab Dad,
Mom of faith,
children should not
bring disgrace.

Praying for life
goodness and love,
in a Greenwich
mosque when young,
only to be shrouded
in hate and a
balaclava hood.

Ready to slice
workers of good,

KKK covered mask,
fire crosses, burned bright,
black instead of white.
Showing off his
shining, serrated knife.

Militant be-header
headless horseman
of fame,
good old Ichabod Crane.

Laying heads
all in a row,
the guillotine had
baskets below.

Heads are rolling,
James Foley,
Alan Henning.

Loving
parents
sorrow
to woe!

TWO STARS

Knifed parents,
head down low
disgraced for having
their son so.

Better to
not know.

Loving
Parents
sorrow
to woe!

The Stoning

Deployed in Afghanistan,
Running alone inside
where I didn't belong.

Hard breezes
as the sand blows
in my face and eyes
a stone hits my temple
"Christ!"

"Allah Akbar" Shouts the boy
as he reloads his sling,
the group
of older men watch,

Smiling,

Rocking,

Nodding,

Saying,

"Mohammed be praised!"

Beloved Child

I saw a girl
crying in the streets,
her beheaded body,
her angelic face,
crying for help,
as I stared and screamed and ran
after her.

Her round head bouncing
up over the rocks,
while the dust
flew over her orb
diamond, rocks encircling,
spilling rocks as stars.
A Queen's Crown.

Her hair as Medusa's,
seducing the roads, beautiful,
long, golden, wavy hair,
sweeps the dirty
streets as a mop,
slops on the kitchen floor.

Blowing up a dust cloud,
to encircle her with a crown,
as the starlit night glimmers
everywhere.
She is laughing now

showing the heathens,
that she was not dead
but alive in Allah.

The laugh was on them
She had beaten
Death!

Overseas Again?

My son tells me
No vacation Mom,
Have orders
Going overseas
Not knowing where.

WHY MINE?

Eating no wings.
This time Mom,
we will do it
at Christmas time.

WHY MINE?

I sit
thinking after
he hangs up.

WHY MINE?

Active Duty

Sunscreen, shampoo,
sanitizer,
bug repellent
floss, mouthwash
Chap Stick!

Things to use
overseas
when deployed,
simple things, donations
to soldiers away from home.

Packing socks, aspirin,
Rice Krispy treats
note cards, pens
puzzles, books.

Seeing the soldier
enjoying the surprise
Christmas packages
in the unbearable heat.
Opened in time for
a trip in the jeep
hummer, tank.

TWO STARS

Send me away,
"Cascade Bouquet!"

Oh, deodorant to kill
the smell of foreign
Isis men, live or die
flaming black.

Sons and daughters
giggling, happy to see
home front sending special
treats that they love to receive.

Groundhog Day

He is overseas,
I know not where
thinking,
day after day
the same?
Up at seven
off at ten.

Run, eat, sleep
and tent again.
Every day begins
the same again.

War games don't wait for them.
Only to do the next day
Again, again and again!

One hundred twenty days
must be gone, for men to
break the cycle of war,
and come home again.

IDF (Israeli Defense Force)

Met on an elevator,
Twenty floors up.
Two striking girls,
One dark, auburn, flowing hair cascading
down her long, young, formed,
hard, toned frame
with curves you would kill for.
Face of angel with ringlets encircling her
Aquiline, perfect, featured face.
She says, "Hello" as we are doing the polite
formalities of life.

"Oh this is my friend, Rachael,
she is the best sharp shooter
in the Israeli Army."
Shocked and surprised,
I hear in reply to my daughter,
"Oh no, you are the
Top Gun pilot
saving all those lives!"

The Girls

Sitting on bar stools
drinking beer and shots,
Chatting away,
long thick hair encircling
their perfect model bodies.
Beautiful girls gabbing.
At an age when friends
weddings are usually
the topic of discussion,
but listen carefully,
theirs is decidedly different!

Unwanted, grabbing hands on their legs,
smacked butts, no toilets on planes.
They use the guy's jar, that's all you need.
One of the few, Military Female Pilots,
harassed it seems?

Disbelief is what I feel.
How can this be in a
world we find real?
Prejudice gone but still

TWO STARS

Good Old Boys, abound?
No room for a girl
to pretty to be around!

The Cats

Two panthers, one dark
with black fluffy fur while the
other is sleek and white with golden hair.
Sitting at a table, two covert blue angels,
Purring over
their past White House,
positions, working
the diplomatic state dinners.

Licking and grooming after
the delicious meal by the chef,
chatting away and talking of
who pulled their cheeks and
patted their derrières.

Quiet ladies of importance,
distinguished warriors,
handpicked as Presidential
Aides, getting ready to run the Marine
Marathon with the best. Sharpening their
claws for protection against
those who always take unwanted allowances.

"Meow!"

Mixed Tea Bags

Mixed bags,
of all types, working together,
Steeping to set it right.
Not knowing,
What will happen today?

Sense of impending
doom for safety sake.
Blown up men and women,
Wounded Warriors, in their place.

Getting a breath of freshness,
from home grown packages,
The desert cold makes foot warmers
heat up blistered feet, remembering fire-pits,
thinking of s'mores to eat.

Boxed collections sent,
deodorant, puzzles, chap stick too,
postage paid love
unknown gift givers
to all mixed teas to see.

Fighting a steaming,
hot spot of mountainous fires.

Flamed feet from shots fired
thinking of Twizzlers, Starbursts
and Trail Mix too.

Love boxes sent with school children's
notes too, saying,

"Thank you soldiers for staying true."

Picture Perfect

Speak to me, I said,
"Why are you here?"
"Can't you see I just landed?"
Barf bag in hand,
Alka Seltzer wasting.

"Why are you here to upset me?"
I see you on the wall and I know you.
Out of thousands of people in an airport
I see you in Uniform, that army
camouflage, that makes you look safe
and healthy.

But I know different.

You are

My Poster Child,

My Wounded Warrior,

for

PTSD.

Three Men

PTSD (Post Traumatic Stress Disorder)

Forward controllers
on the ground, one radioing
"Help!"
Now home, at fancy "DC" bar,
West Pointers, out
drinking their old lives away
with tequila shots today.
All three, out to dinner trying
to be normal, cool,
enjoying being seen.
Flirting with girls
but afraid to be at liberty
of tics and looking over
one's shoulders to see,
who is around?
or escaping free?

A Little Twinkle

They light the spot,
stars, full of brilliance,
burning ever so bright.
Palm trees wait
for the passing storm,
bending heavy heads
to the pavement
never breaking,
until they come home.
Gale winds orbiting their heads,
as they dance and scream
in sounds of wailing
"Are they alive or dead?"
Their hair circling over,
bending ever more
until they touch the ground,
crying, sighing together
in a chorus of hurricane winds,
hysterically moaning but never
breaking in two.
Bright stars come home,
the storm is over.
We are waiting for the voices of
children coming home

from the danger zones.
Unnecessary wars,
taking lives of sons and
daughter.
Some captured and beheaded,
scars unheralded in hearts so brave,
wondering will they be saved?

Grandma, I Am Home

She kneels and digs her nails
working the fruitful earth.
Her ninety year old arthritic body,
a women of Faith. Grace, Love and
Beauty.

The face with the lines of a woman of
tenderness and understanding,
have been through
many losses in life.
So she digs her new garden as done
fifty years ago,
pulling the beautiful wormy weeds
to let the seeds grow full and strong.

He has grown into a man
of twenty one,
strong and handsome with
talents beyond words
but with a weed that
grew within his being
to twist his mind
and life.

Never to marry he says
as he is sick with the disease
that is unspoken.
He watches from a distance
as she prunes her vines
perfuming the full odor
of ripened abundance.
But his snare is twisted by his own
misgiving and questions that
make him wonder.

Never knowing peace,
his silent screams to
a silent, un-answering God.

Only to hear nothing from
anyone. Quiet is the killer.
No one to listen or see this
broken soul?

As she looks back at her
work and smiles, she feels
his warm glance staring, from the
bridge of no return.
She turns looking at the uniformed man
As he says,
"Grandma I'm home"

TWO STARS

She is thinking of how he has
grown into a strong confident man,
not seeing that he
is climbing the rail
to leap to his end.

Mamma, May I?

(To a dear friend who lost her grandson by suicide)

The bee sees its target and
flies around for awhile
hoping it will be there,
but he knows that he can't
attack until he goes to the nest
and requests permission.

He flies in and asks the Queen,
who is very busy with her own needs,
making her nest and worried about the
others who are after her position and power.
She is thinking nothing of the dangers that her loyal drone has
encountered.

He does his radio dance
around and around and he
knows what must be done
to protect the nest but she is
too busy protecting her own status
not caring about the soldier drone.

TWO STARS

He leaves with an unanswered
request and hears static
while he takes off to protect
the colony. He circles
getting ready for the big battle to attack
the infidels.

Politics be what they are,
he is told to "Stand Down",
"Wait for orders." while
he gets shot down,
diving down to his death.

War Eagles

(Winds of War)

World War I, II
Pearl harbor
Vietnam
Afghanistan.

Why can't we learn
from the past?
Go on to see what a peaceful future
will bring?

Same mistakes,
misreading history,
only to repeat deaths
of the innocent young.

To fulfill
the power hungry men,
in political forums.
Have you never
learned?

TWO STARS

Life is sacred.
Are you all so
blind to see
History?

Repeat!
Repeat!
Repeat!

Blue Angels

They fly as if their
pants are on fire!
Doing flybys so low your
ears explode as they come overhead
and whiz by with that Mach Five speed.
The ground rumbles and roars back
to echo their sound breaking booms,
thundering down out of nowhere
crisscrossing and straight up again.

They are the Hornets of the Sky,
liberating the music of the winds.
To do a show that beats all others,
the Fleur di Leis, the barrel roll,
wing to wing by eighteen.
close enough to meet whites of eyes.
Stunts unbelievable to be seen,
defying gravity as one.

TWO STARS

Daedalus demonstrating to Icarus
how to do it right
and not get too close.
Burning the airways with
contrails that can be seen for miles
only to hear him them come rumbling
down the run-way.

A hornet at mach speed,
four-five g's of pressure before
you pass out.
Perfect precision and flying as of old
wingtip to wingtip.

Little did we know that on
the very next show,
one will "put out his hand and touch the
face of God."

They have a motto that never leaves
them.

US Navy Blue Angles
They have a motto that never leaves them "Once a Blue Angel, always a Blue Angel."

Spirit Uprising

I watched a man die as an angel
swept him up into the heavens,
the wind sweeping up the dirt into a funnel,
carrying away the soul, sand, dirt in a whirlwind.

The spirit body purified from the sand and
dirt as if life's living was tainted.

Given to a
Radiant
Star
Brilliantly shining gold, refined,
assayed of all earthly impurities.

Bellowing silent sounds
of deep anguish
for leaving life, he is released.
His tarnished soul
redefined as my
Guardian Angel.

(For Norman, my gentle smiling soul.)

The Dark Life

D is the denseness,
A is the awful feelings of being lost,
R is for running away from terrible pain,
K is for the kneeling deathbed to take it all away.

L is for the lost life so sadly missed,
I for the invisible person,
F is for forgiven soul,
E is for the energy gone.

The Cemetery

Life living
Life loving
Life giving
Life gone.

Flags flying
over grass
saying singing warriors
you fought the last.

We remember
smiles and laughter
sadness shadowing
a life hereafter.

Arlington National Cemetery

Taps

(Blown Away)

Picnicking on the carpet of grass,
on a breezy, sunny, warm, balmy day.
Hearing the sound of illegitimate clinking
wine glasses toasting a life long gone.

Rocks propped on top of marble,
remembrances of love and lives.
Hearing the laughter of others,
doing the same, then tears of a missed smile.

Bugles in the distance,
playing their woeful song
of farewell, reminding
of another hero's goodbye.

TWO STARS

Funeral fly-by in missing plane formation, one plane missing for the fallen

Transcendence

Walking eyes open/shut,
from a fitful dream,
of spirits long gone
in cemetery seams.

Walking at Arlington,
feeling feet groveling in forest grass.
Grassy little chubby fingers grabbing my
feet with tiny curly green hands.

Tired of fighting the knobby green turf
I drop down to my knees,
kneeling, contemplating
with an eyeless stare,
at a transcendent door to nowhere.

Supercilious, glorious, radiant streams
of various hues of golden light,
framing the doors edges.
Beckoning me,
to float to the other side.

TWO STARS

Taken aback, I hear
the echoing sounds
in my head so clear,
of whispers and laughter
Celestial music ever so near.
Glued to the floor,

immobilized,
sounds saying,
"Go back not your time yet."

Unconscious I walk
to a bed so bare,
cover with a sheet
to hear no more,
but remembering all.

Rock

You were the one
who kept us together,
the rock that anchored
the ships in the storms of life.

The son lost from PTSD,
no model to follow,
the daughter putting off her life,
to care for a grieving lost mother.

Walking on Scruffy Turf

In Arlington cemetery,
ever wonder
what it would be like
to lie on a grave
arms folded ever so gently
and slide falling lightly into a grave
of a loved one
and slip into their
silent sleeping body
cold and stiff
long dead
Feel the warmth
radiating from you to them
getting that last bit of breath
Breathing slowly
Life ebbing like the waves on the ocean
Up and down
Back and forth
A gentle breeze of snoring
Come back my love
return the warmth of those kisses

Let me feel the arms caressing my lonely body
But I can't even remember your face
long gone as the sun
Set at night
your return is the dawn of resurrection
until the light filters
radiantly through the doors edges
until a hand reaches down for mine.

Arlington

We ride
behind the
funeral procession,
six horses,
click clacking,
on the Cobblestones
Perfect rhythms slowly
gracefully sashaying,
tails swatting flies.

Headstones in perfect unison,
neatly checker boarded rows,
lines down a hill.
The last
resting place of
a loving Vietnam
pilot,
husband,
soldier,
father,
friend.

Gut wrenching sobs,
silent screams,
quiet air.
The deafening twenty-one gun salute,
on a dark cloudy day.

Horse's clip clop, clip clop,
the parade marches
on a spring, cherry, blossom day.
Wagon on its way
gets closer to
six in, two over.

Stopping at
the final,
resting place.
As roaring jets,
do a flyby formation.
One plane missing,
as Clydesdale's droppings
dance in perfect timing to taps!
Erupting the mood breaking,
uncontrollable, hysterical laughter!
He saying,
"Be happy
gone away.
Day is done."

TWO STARS

Funeral procession, Arlington National Cemetery

Poppies

They blow in the breezes
swaying with a lifelong gone.
Telling each other stories of war and
life that is buried below,
from a long, long time ago.

The men who lived and battled
still wonder was the good fight fought?
Are we still protecting those ideals?
Of freedom and democracy?
Or are our lives gone in vain?

The poppies still blow red in
the breeze as men sell them
on wire stems,
blood red to remind us,
Freedom is not free.

Profits from the sale of the book will be donated to the Rivers of Recovery.

VICTORIA VENTURA

Order Form

Number of books: _____

Name: _____

Address:
_____
_____
_____

Phone: _____ Email: _____

Two Stars:
Reflections of a Military Wife and Mother

ISBN: *978-0-9978562-4-8*

Mail checks to:
Victoria Ventura
258 Opening Hill Road
Madison, CT 06443-1921

www.ingramcontent.com/pod-product-compliance
Lightning Source LLC
Chambersburg PA
CBHW080413300426
44113CB00015B/2508